Fables & Folktales

The Ants & the Grasshopper

By Tyler Gieseke

Dash!
LEVELED READERS
An Imprint of Abdo Zoom • abdobooks.com

Level 1 – Beginning
Short and simple sentences with familiar words or patterns for children who are beginning to understand how letters and sounds go together.

Level 2 – Emerging
Longer words and sentences with more complex language patterns for readers who are practicing common words and letter sounds.

Level 3 – Transitional
More developed language and vocabulary for readers who are becoming more independent.

abdobooks.com

Published by Abdo Zoom, a division of ABDO, PO Box 398166, Minneapolis, Minnesota 55439.

Printed in the United States of America, North Mankato, Minnesota.
102025
012026

Photo Credits: ABDO, Artistly, Shutterstock
Production Contributors: Jennie Forsberg, Grace Hansen, Tyler Gieseke
Design Contributors: Candice Keimig, Neil Klinepier, Colleen McLaren

Library of Congress Control Number: 2025936785

Publisher's Cataloging in Publication Data

Names: Gieseke, Tyler, author.
Title: The ants & the grasshopper / by Tyler Gieseke
Description: Minneapolis, Minnesota : Abdo Zoom, 2026 | Series: Fables & folktales | Includes online resources and index.
Identifiers: ISBN 9798384940029 (lib. bdg.) | ISBN 9798384940784 (ebook) | ISBN 9798384941163 (read-to-me ebook)
Subjects: LCSH: Insects--Juvenile literature. | Aesop's fables--Juvenile literature. | Work ethic--Juvenile literature. | Conduct of life--Juvenile literature. | Character development--Juvenile literature. | Problem solving--Juvenile literature. | Procrastination--Juvenile literature. | Fables--Juvenile literature.
Classification: DDC 398.2 [E]--dc23

Table of Contents

Fables & Folktales

Fables and folktales are both kinds of stories. Fables are usually short. They teach a clear **lesson**. They often include talking animals.

Folktales are **traditional** stories that come from a group of people. Adults often pass down these stories to children.

The Ants & the Grasshopper

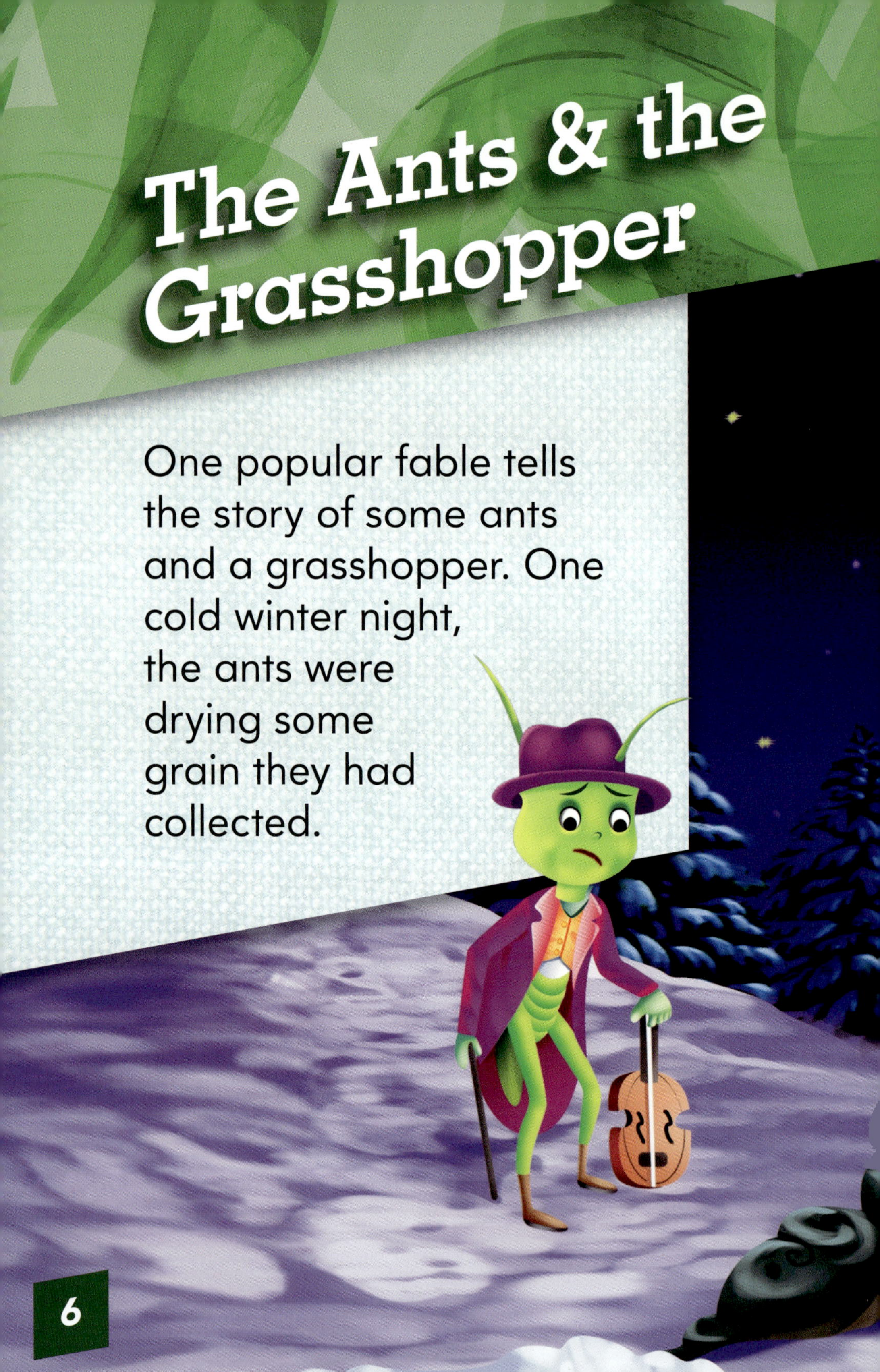

One popular fable tells the story of some ants and a grasshopper. One cold winter night, the ants were drying some grain they had collected.

While they were doing this, a grasshopper approached them. He was shaking with hunger.

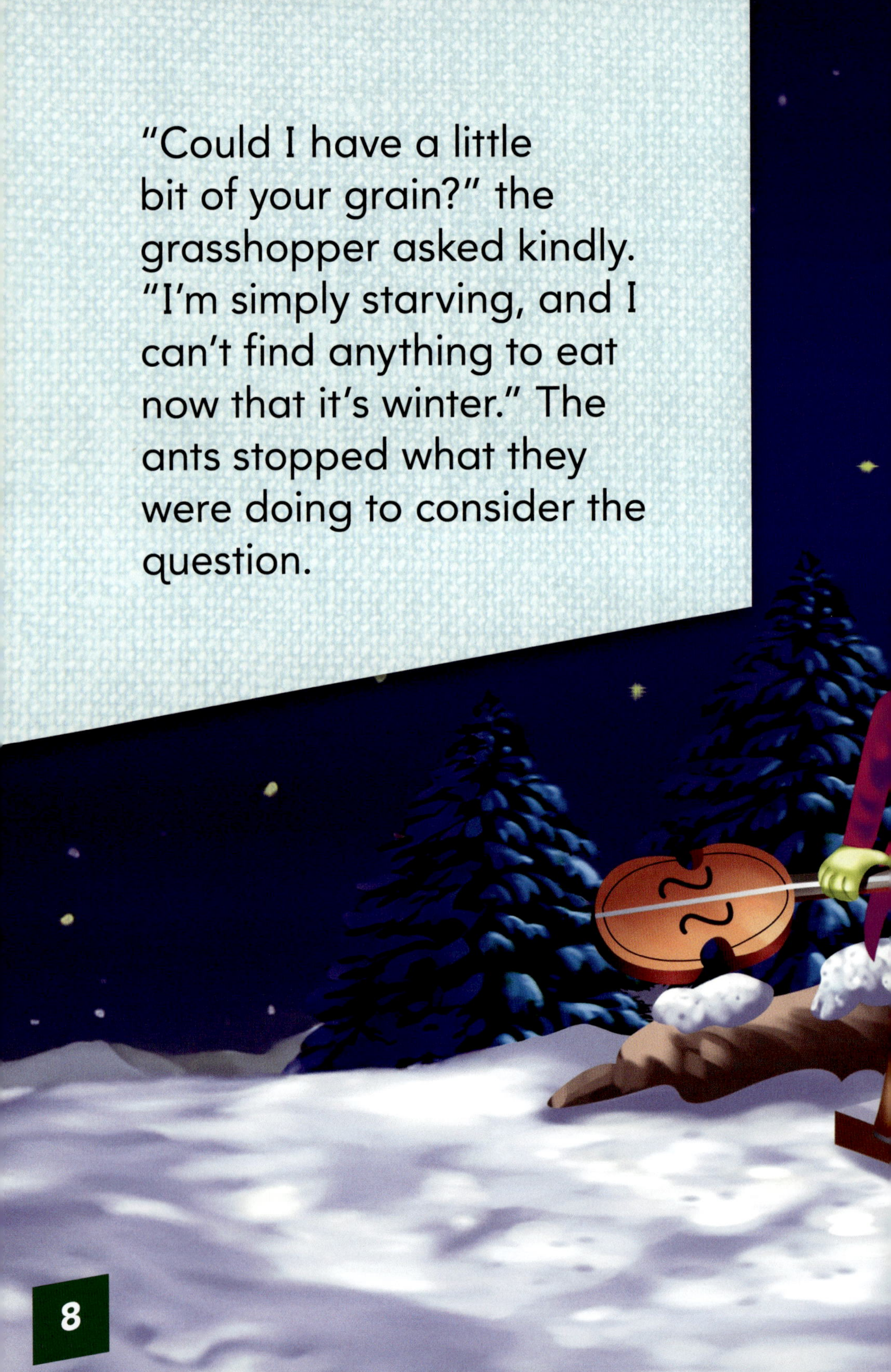

"Could I have a little bit of your grain?" the grasshopper asked kindly. "I'm simply starving, and I can't find anything to eat now that it's winter." The ants stopped what they were doing to consider the question.

"Can we ask you what you were doing all last summer?" the ants said in reply. "Why haven't you stored up any food, as we have? Didn't you know winter was coming?"

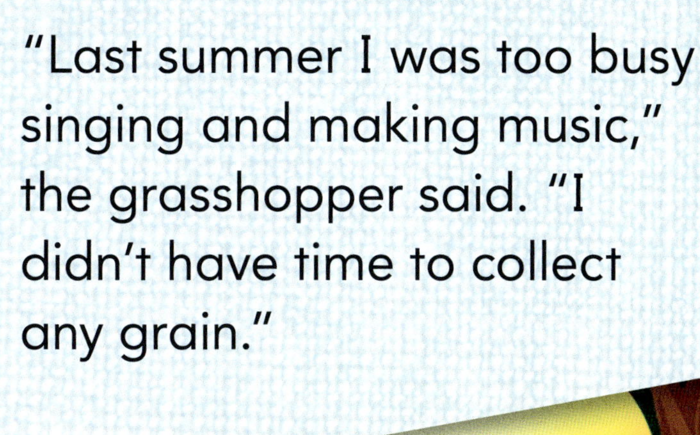

"Last summer I was too busy singing and making music," the grasshopper said. "I didn't have time to collect any grain."

Hearing this, the ants laughed at the grasshopper. "You were too busy singing, were you?" they said. "Well, if you sang in the summer, you must now dance in the winter!" And they turned back to their work.

The grasshopper went away very hungry. He thought that the ants were probably right—there is both a time for work and a time for play.

Lessons

The **moral** of this fable is that there is a time for work and a time for play. It's important to make time for both. If people play all the time, like the grasshopper did during the summer, they will miss out on the basics of life. But if people work all the time, maybe like the ants, life will be boring and dull.

Balancing work and play doesn't have to be hard. One example would be to get homework done before going out to play sports. Another would be to **avoid** playing video games for the entire day if there are chores to do. Both having fun and working hard are key.

A second **lesson** of the fable is that not every day is sunny. It's best to be prepared for all times. The ants know that winter will come. So, they store grain and have food for hard times. The grasshopper is prepared only for the best of times, and he suffers for it.

Education
Sa

If you earn an **allowance**, you might not want to spend all the money right away. Like the ants, you can save some of it for when you need it. Maybe there will come a week or a month when your parents can't give you an allowance. But you will still have some money saved up!

More Facts

- *The Ants & the Grasshopper* is one of Aesop's fables. These are a famous collection of fables believed to have been written by Aesop.

- Aesop is believed to have been a slave from ancient Greece who later became free. He lived from about 620 to 564 BCE.

- But there are many different versions of Aesop's life and where he came from. Some people even believe Aesop never existed! They think he was made up.

- Pixar's 1998 film *A Bug's Life* was partly based off *The Ants & the Grasshopper.*

Glossary

allowance – a small amount of money some parents regularly give their children.

avoid – to stay away from something.

balance – to arrange things so that they work well together.

lesson – a teaching, or something learned.

moral – a teaching to take away from a story.

traditional – describing something done regularly and over time by a group of people.

Index

Online Resources

To learn more about *The Ants & the Grasshopper*, please visit **abdobooklinks.com** or scan this QR code. These links are routinely monitored and updated to provide the most current information available.